Jimmy Jock
Six-Sided Clock Albert and the

First Published in 1993 by
Cornerhouse Publications
70 Oxford Street
Manchester M1 5NH
061 228 7621

ISBN 0948797 62 2

Design and Artwork Production: Cornerhouse
Prints: Charlie Meecham
Reprographics: Leeds Photo Litho
Print: Jackson Wilson

The staff at Cornerhouse for
Jimmy Jock, Albert and the Six-Sided Clock:
Dewi Lewis, Director
Niall Allsop, Design & Production
Stephanie Laidler, Production Assistant
Alison Buchan, Sales & Distribution
A complete catalogue of Cornerhouse Publications is available on request

Published in association with National Museums & Galleries on Merseyside to coincide with
the exhibition *Jimmy Jock, Albert and the Six-Sided Clock* at Merseyside Maritime Museum,
21 May – 5 September, 1993

This book has been made possible with the financial support of National Museums & Galleries
on Merseyside, Northern Arts and the Arts Council of Great Britain

Jimmy Jock Albert and the Six-Sided Clock

Photographs of Liverpool's Docklands
by John Darwell

C Cornerhouse Publications
in association with
National Museums & Galleries on Merseyside

Thanks to …

Tony Tibbles, Curator Maritime History, Maritime Museum
for his faith in and support for this project

MDHB in particular Kathryn Jones for help and access

Pauline, Carol and Joan at YWCA for their hospitality

Stockport College of Further Education for making contact printing easy

Angie for putting up with morning sickness and the dogs

Dad for innumerable trips up the M6 to check on my rapidly expanding family

Mum for letting him

The people of Merseyside for being as honest and forthright as I had expected

C Type prints by Charlie Meecham, Outsiders Photography

John Bradshaw, Dewi Lewis and Niall Allsop

For Angela, Lucy and Matthew

The Port of Liverpool for centuries has been synonymous with seafaring. Much of the city bears witness to this proud (and not so proud!) past in its buildings, monuments and street names.

Today the port is undergoing great changes; the vast legions of dockers are now all but gone, taking with them the pubs and cafés along the dock road, the process of visible decline obscuring the fact that the turnover of the port is now at record levels. Mechanisation has left many areas of dockland as empty reminders of what once was, the giant cranes stand disused or in the throes of dismantling – an adventure playground par excellence for the local kids.

On exploring the docks you still come under the scrutiny of the port police – often the only people to be found in the more out of the way areas. I watched one policeman spend an afternoon guarding the gates whilst lovingly washing his car, such was the activity taking place that day.

The men who remain working the port are proud of their tradition, their caustic wit still flying around the graving docks, but the men are getting older and the jobs fewer – what apprentices there are have to look for work elsewhere once out of their time. They still get sent for a long weight (wait) or an air hook, but things move on and the age of the push button is replacing the camaraderie and skills of yesterday. "It's not Jimmy it's Jimmy Jock" resounding through the ship – but for how much longer?

Maritime Museum, Large Exhibits Store, now closed to public

On the more run down dock sites, grass and brambles grow on areas of former activity, preparing the way for the bull dozers that will inevitably alter the face of the area forever in the move towards leisure and tourism.

Marinas and shopping centres stand poised on drawing boards awaiting an 'upturn in the economy' – that favourite phrase of government politicians. The corridors of Albert resound to the tramp of browsing tourists, "not buying, just looking", peering into the Granada Studios - "is that Richard and Judy? – I can't see very well – wave, we might be on telly!" or munching through overpriced exotic snacks, awaiting the arrival of Fred (a TV weatherman) – known even to Kings and Queens – the power of celebrity!

Back on the dock front one ritual that never changes. Every evening the prostitutes sneak into the port, the word's out a ship's in and it's not only the engines that need servicing. Though the crews are mainly form the third world and speak no English the universal language prevails!

What will happen to the port and its remaining workers in years to come? Will we see dockers trooping down to the ships once again? Moving cargo, not for real but for us the onlookers, whilst the 'real' work goes on two miles down the road in the world of 'high tech' containers moved by robots. Will the old docks follow the cotton industry and mines into the glorified never never land of the heritage industry? Only time will tell.

Jimmy Jock

Albert and the Six-Sided Clock

Canteen, Seaforth Container Base

"They're not what they used to be."

Demolition, Gladstone Dock

"When they put these up they thought they were there for ever."

Gladstone Dock

Gladstone Dock

Gladstone Dock with Korean-bound scrap metal ship under tow

Tugs turning freighter, Gladstone Dock

Removing roof cranes prior to demolition, Gladstone Dock

Attaching cables to 'Mersey Mammoth' – Europe's largest floating crane

Last crane going over the edge, Gladstone Dock

Animal Feeds Berth, Canada Dock

"We had someone down here with a new video camera last week – after a morning here it never worked again!"

Silo Operator, Animal Feedstuffs, Canada Dock

Silo Operator, Canada Dock

Loading animal feed, Canada Dock

Seaman 'Dimitrakis', Animal Feeds Berth, Canada Dock

"One day they gave us all little brushes and pans and said 'go and sweep those tyres' – hundreds of them – can you believe it!"

Cleaning sludge from graving dock, Branch Dock No 1, Canada Dock

"We hadn't got the plans for this ship that was due in dry dock – we were going to guess its bow shape for the support blocks – then this lad says 'hang on I'll be back in twenty minutes' – comes back with a full set of photocopied plans – turns out he had plans for any ship you could think of stored in his loft!"

Welders, Trafalgar Graving Dock

Welding prop' cover, Trafalgar Graving Dock

Refitting prop' and rudder to 'Vigilant', Trafalgar Graving Dock

"Once the ship is finished a good many of these lads will be back on the dole –
most of them are too old to change their ways now."

Scalers taking a break, 'Vigilant', Trafalgar Graving Dock

When you were doing the oil tanks, there was no such thing as protective clothing then, you just went in the way you were. It was crude oil and it used to cling and smell. When I got home I had to take my clothes off on the step, wrap them up and then just go in the way I was. My mother would have a bath ready. There was no such thing as laundrettes then, you just had to clean them the best way you could. Of course she didn't have a washing machine, so they had to be done in the bath. When she was done I had to clean the oil off the bath. When you worked on oil tankers you'd get what they called time and fifty. If you worked eight hours in an oil tanker you'd get paid for twelve hours. The money was obviously for the damage that it was doing to your clothes because you'd only need four jobs on an oil tanker and you'd have to throw them away. The crude oil used to rot them.

Tom Fairbrother, Scaler, late 1940s
from *The Mersey Ship Repairers* by Ken Moore

Scaler ready for work, 'Vigilant', Trafalgar Dock

We had to go down into the fresh water tanks and chip all the old cement wash off with a hammer. They were hard to get into because you had to climb through openings like port-holes without the glass, it was very awkward. When you finished chipping away you put all the old cement in a bucket and sent it through. The man at the far end would pass through buckets of fresh cement wash and we'd brush decks, sides and the bulk-head, and then move onto another tank ... The crawling was the hardest part. The tanks were only a few feet high so that you had to work in a bent over position like Quasimodo, The Hunchback of Notre Dame.

Tom Fairbrother 1947
from *The Mersey Ship Repairers* by Kevin Moore

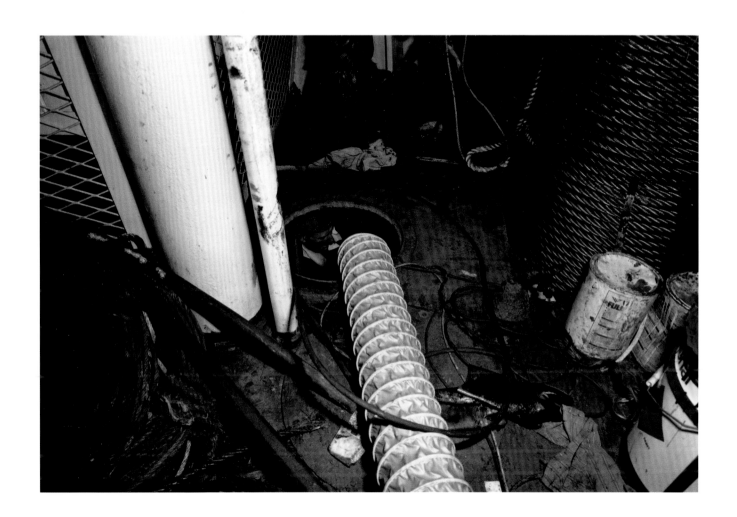

Scaler at work, 'Vigilant'

"You should've photographed it last week – then we could've seen how it went back together."

Engine Room, 'Vigilant'

The foreman would come to you at 2 minutes to 5 and say 'you, you and you get back here at 7 o'clock, you're working all night.' 'Mr Clarkson, I'm going to night school tonight.' 'Not tonight you're not, you're working for us, be back here for 7 o'clock.' You didn't argue with him. You'd go home, have your dinner, get fresh sandwiches, a fresh brew of tea, one for your supper and one for your breakfast, and then you'd go back. At 7 o'clock you'd go down to the Langton Dock, the graving dock where the ship was lying. It would probably be a job where you would have to take the propeller off, which could weigh anything up to twenty tons. You'd work from 7 o'clock till midnight and then you'd go for your supper which was 12 till half past 12. Then you'd work through; until 7 o'clock the following morning and then go for your breakfast. I was telling a young fella this once and he said to me 'Ah, then you'd go home.' I said 'Oh, no you didn't, you started a fresh day's work.'

Leslie I Anson late 1940s

from *The Mersey Ship Repairers* by Kevin Moore

Ship loading scrap metal, Canada Dock

Because of limited manoeuvring ability of large ships it can take over half a
working day to drag a ship 200 metres by hand, thus gaining
access to rear hold areas.

.

Towing ship along quayside, Canada Dock

Towing 'Norman Supreme', lorry driver 'supervising', Canada Dock

"It leaves as scrap, comes back as steel."

Loading scrap metal, Canada Dock

Huskisson Dock

"One lad put a welding torch through one of these – full of gas it killed him
and his mate – just like a bomb going off."

•

Scraping barnacles and rust off Mersey buoys, Huskisson Dock

"It's going to become one huge coal depot – the power stations would rather
buy from abroad – low sulphur coal, saves them having to
clean up their own systems."

.

Coal loading area, Gladstone Dock

"New facilities will increase coal imports from 2 million tonnes to over 5 million. Development will be subject to agreement with Sefton Council who took coal importers to court after complaints from local residents about drifting coal dust."

Coal storage site, Freeport area, Gladstone Dock

Scrap metal 'swarf' awaiting export, Gladstone Dock

Korean bound scrap metal, Gladstone Dock

"Some of the cars we drive off the Atlantic ships are beautiful – we had Elvis' car here – all the lads would sit in it and have their photos taken. Some of the cars, you only find out they've no brakes when you're halfway down the ramp – then you're shouting 'get out the bloody way."

"Dropped a container onto this guy some time ago – could only tell who it was
'cos one hand was sticking out from underneath – it had a ring on it!"

Loading container onto lorry, Royal Seaforth Container Terminal

Awaiting docking of 'Atlantic Conveyer' where boyfriends and brothers are crewmen, Seaforth Container Terminal

Docker, Seaforth Terminal

Seaforth Container Terminal

View from grain tower, across lorry park, to Bootle Housing Estate

Seen in dockland pub:

"Due to the high cost of water, beer in here will now be at full strength."

"We've been selling here for over 15 years – it used to be all dockers – now it's
mostly housewives driving into town."

Fish seller, Regent (Dock) Road

"You see young kids climbing all over these things – you daren't shout at them in case they get distracted and fall off."

Council houses facing docks, Derby Road Estate, Bootle

New housing, Seaforth

"'Cos we supported the miners she was out to get us – and she did!"

.

Club house, Seaforth

Jimmy Jock **Albert** and the Six-Sided Clock

World of Animation, Albert Dock

'The Beatles Story'

Candle Maker

"Most people don't want to buy, they just come on the coach for a look around
– they bring 30p with them for a cup of tea!"

Window display

Bags for sale

"They talk about all the people who come here but half the cars out there are
'cos it's free parking and they can walk into town."

·

Poster seller

Maritime prints

South American chimes

"It becomes a vicious circle, once people start to close down the word goes out that all the shops are closing and people stop coming."

Empty shop

"You should be here at 12 o'clock when Fred (a weatherman) comes out, the docks are lined with people – then they all disappear!"

Fred – cut-out of a weatherman

Jimmy Jock Albert and the Six-Sided Clock

Derelict warehouse, Princess Half Tide Dock, looking to the Cunard/Liver Buildings

Looking across Collingwood and Salisbury Docks to old bonded tea warehouse, 'Three Sisters' power station, Cantilever bridge and the Six-Sided Clock – all disused!

Derelict warehouse, Princess Half Tide Dock

Vittoria Dock, Birkenhead

Gary, Morpeth Dock. Hoping proposed redevelopment will help his marina to become a success

Morpeth Dock, Birkenhead

Derelict cranes, Bidston Dock looking to West Float, Birkenhead

Bidston Dock, disused – used as adventure playground by local children

"Today fewer than ten men work the entire Birkenhead dock system from Alfred to Bidston. In 1920 there were thirty-six dock gate men, four head gate men and five pier masters at Alfred alone."

A Johnston
Working the Tides

Bidston Dock, Birkenhead

Houses adjacent to derelict dockland, West Float, Birkenhead

Derelict corn warehouses, East Float, Birkenhead

We still have a look, Joyce and I, when we come along the dock road by car, we slow
down and have a look. I've even been round the back and had a poke around, having a
look where this was and trying to recognise where that was, it's very nostalgic.
The convivial pub is still on the corner, where Browns was is now a car park, but if
you look at the wall you can see where the chimney breast comes up the fireplace.
I know the exact spot against the wall where we used to sit by the fireplace, you can
picture it, even though the building is gone.

John Thompson on A R Browns
from *The Mersey Ship Repairers* by Kevin Moore

Empty pub, Waterloo Road/Regent Road – main dock road – on recent visit to area someone had 'removed' the sign and letters from pub

Morpeth Dock

East Float

"You know this Government pushed the abolition of dock labour scheme through in a week – it was the quickest bill ever to go through!"

Disused canteen, Hornby Dock

"They used to take us dockers to one side on Friday night and say 'come back Monday and we'll pay you for the weekend' – they had their own lads and didn't need us, but the union said there had to be so many dockers on each job, it was called 'ghosting' – really we helped cut our own throats!"

Seaforth, looking along Mersey Estuary

When this project was first discussed between myself and the merseyside
Maritime Museum, my mental picture of the docklands was one of cranes,
ships and men at work. The cranes and ships are still there but the men have
mostly disappeared. At its peak, more than 20,000 men were employed on the
docks alone. Now less than 600 men work the entire dockland system.
Ironically the amount of cargo passing through the docks is at record levels,
mechanisation having replaced man as the main transporter. Often the only
people to be found were several hundred feet up operating container cranes
and transporters. What people I did find were either extremely friendly and
interested in what I was doing, or were highly suspicious of my motives – years
of bad press seem to have given many Merseysiders a justified wariness when
it comes to the media.

The docks are thriving. Can this prosperity be justified in terms of jobs lost?

John Darwell
April 1993

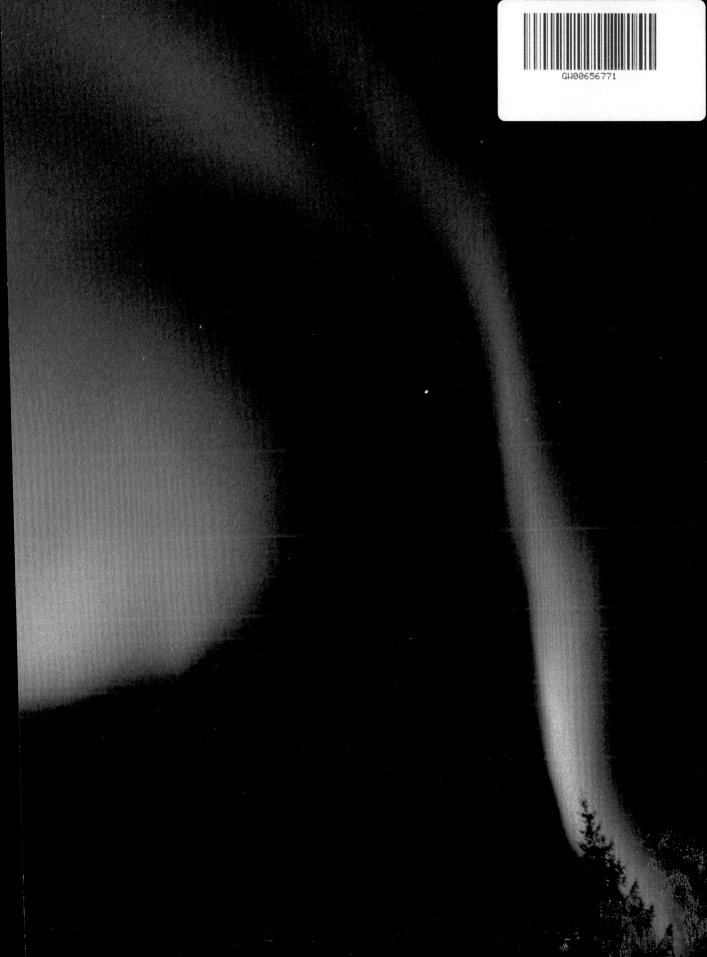

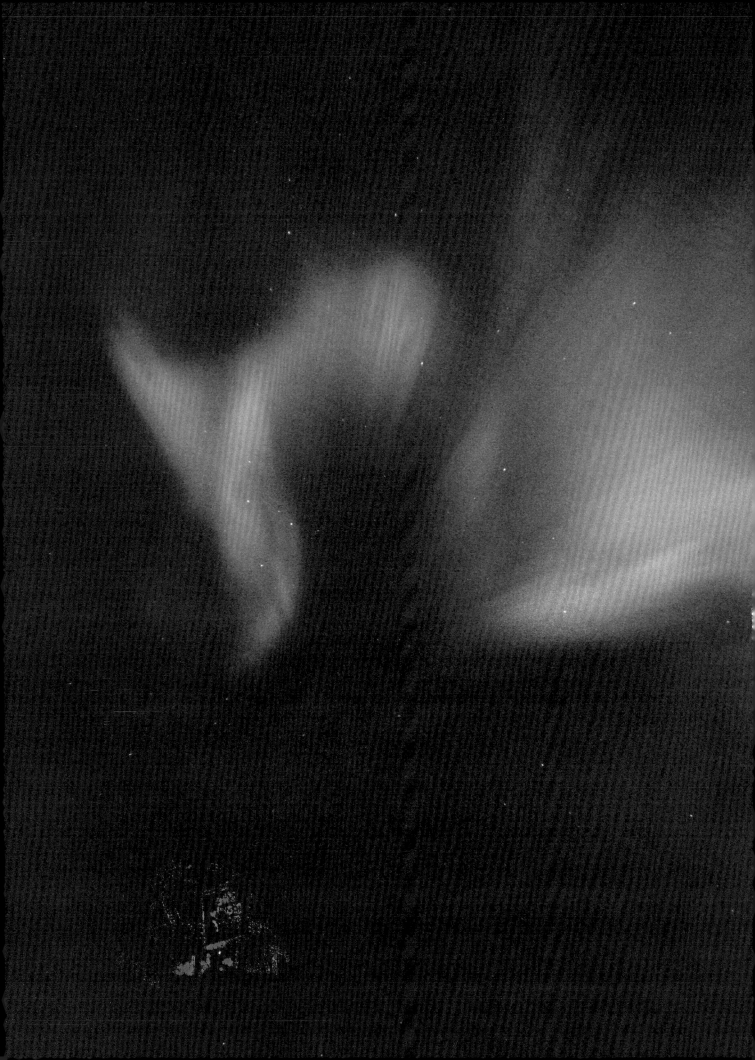

Winter
on the Finnish Taiga

Hannu Hautala

Winter
on the Finnish Taiga

Otava Publishing Company Ltd.

Translation:
Malcolm Hicks

Design and layout:
Markku Tanttu

3rd edition

Paper:
Galerie Art 150 g/m^2
Colour separation, typesetting and printing:
Kaleva Printing Company,
Oulu 1999
Binding:
Otava Book Printing Co.,
Keuruu 1999

ISBN 951-1-11264-3

The taiga, the northern coniferous forest zone, covers a vast area thousands of kilometres wide extending from Finland right across to the Pacific Ocean.

The forest landscapes of Finland have many typical taiga features. The steep hill slopes of the Kuusamo area, for instance, with their stately candle spruces shaped by the cold winters and the weight of snow on their branches, or the fauna of the same Koillismaa region, animals which have adapted to the severe cold, the shortage of light and the accumulation of snow.

The first snow can easily fall while the autumn leaves are still in full colour.

The gold of the leaves blends with the white of the snow.

Summer in the taiga has given way to winter.

The warmth of the autumn colours on the ground and the sparkling white snow combine to create a feast of brilliance, and the Siberian jay merges with this background as it goes on busily gathering food for the arctic winter.

The stores it is building up among the branches of the trees and in cracks in their bark are essential for survival during the harsh winter ahead.

Most of the migratory birds have left several weeks ago. The forest has plunged into autumn silence.

A dipper has arrived from its nesting grounds on the fjells of Lapland to spend the winter beside the as yet unfrozen streams of Koillismaa. Other birds of the same species which have been nesting here have in turn left on their autumn migration towards the southeast.

The nutcracker, an inhabitant of the Siberian taiga, is an occasional autumn visitor to the cone forests of Koillismaa, while the swan is a regular summer dweller, now preparing for its long journey south as the last of the smaller lakes begin to freeze over.

A warmer day, with temperatures above zero, a reminder of the nearness of the past summer, melts the snow again. But the water is soon frozen by the colder air at night. The home of the Siberian jay, at one moment glowing in its autumn colours, will soon be a grey world, cold and icy.

The winds sprinkle the hills and wooded valleys with new snow.

The crested tit, faithful to the forests which make up its home is hurrying about the task of finding food in this snowy landscape so that one would barely notice it. Even though we may hear its cheerful song, the bird itself is difficult to spot among the branches of a dead, fallen pine.

The magpies have gathered together in flocks once more, and the ravens are also gathering after their summer family life in the more remote corners of the forest. Both prefer to be close to human habitation during the winter.

The moon rises to light up the frosty night, now growing very much longer than the day.

The dipper finds its patches of open water shrinking as the cold becomes more intense.

When no snow falls in the autumn the streams freeze down to their beds
and the oncoming water has to seek out new channels. The result is that
the most surprising spots in the terrain can be covered with a metre or
more of ice, and a tiny stream pouring over a steep rock face can generate
a massive ice colonnade.

Some black is to be seen among the white: evidence
of the presence of life amidst the harsh world of
snow and ice. The unfrozen rim around the hole of
a black woodpecker shows that its inhabitant has

spent the night there, while a raven looks down from its vantage point and sees everything that is moving about in this white world.

A squirrel stands still and tries to escape the gaze of predators, but eventually hunger and cold force it into action even though the danger is still present. It can scarcely have escaped the notice of the eagle.

The snow grows deeper and the frost more intense.

It is midwinter, the darkest time of the year, when daylight lasts for no more than two or three hours.

The fleeting moments of daylight and dusk which punctuate the almost continuous darkness allow the great spotted woodpecker to busy itself with its cones and the crested tit to hunt among the tangled branches in the hope of finding enough food and energy to keep them warm through the cold night. Even after the sun has gone down the woodpecker is still collecting cones to knock the seeds out of them for its supper.

Most days in the middle of winter are cloudy, but occasionally the sun appears above the horizon for a moment and scatters its rays on the forest-clad hilltops. The slopes, valleys and gorges are still a land of shadows.

A ray of sun tinges the harsh winter world of the Siberian tit and Siberian jay with gold, a momentary promise of spring. But these tiny balls of feathers still have several months of frosty winds and chilling snowstorms to survive.

Hunger takes no account of the weather, and drives the wolverine on an insatiable hunting foray.

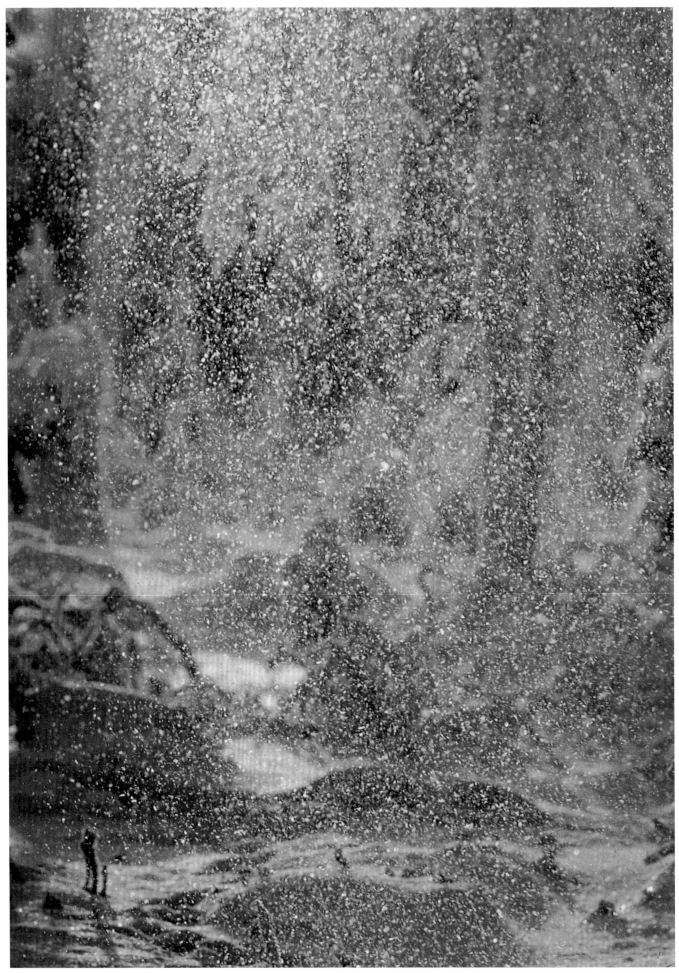

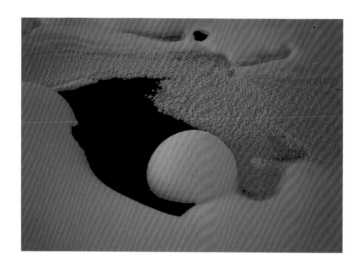

The flowing water of a stream releases its fiery
breath into the crisp, frosty air.

Midwinter is a dark time of year, but not devoid of colour. Even the night sky is lit up by the many hues of the northern lights, like reflections in a pearly mirror, and the daylight, with its frosty mist creates a display of lighting effects that is alive and changing with every minute.

Even the rising moon can vary its colour.

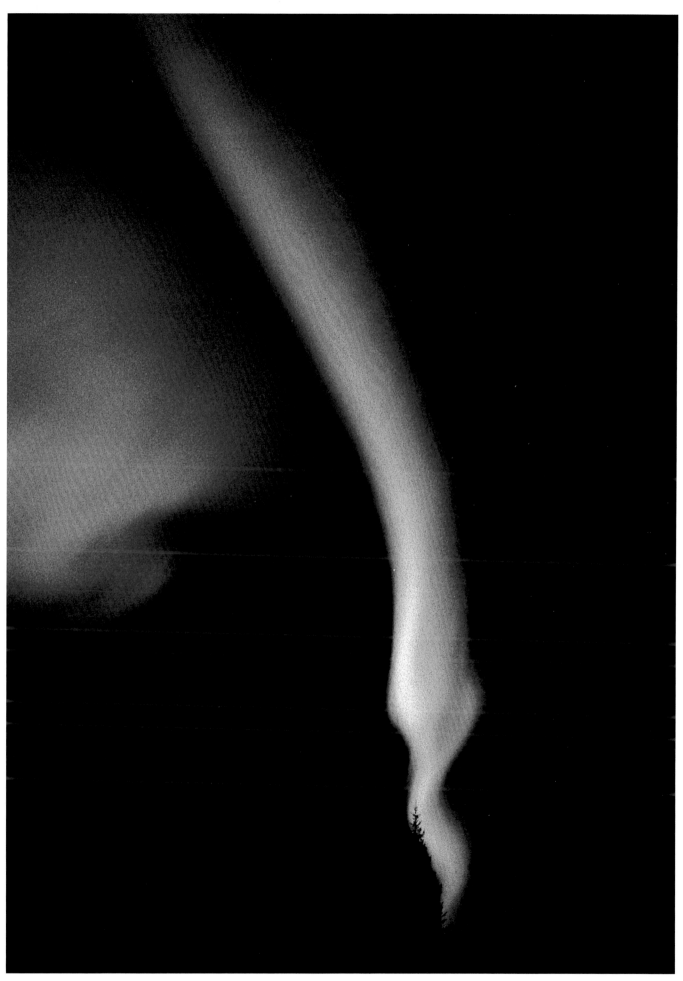

The clouds of frosty mist crystallize out over the trees on the hilltops, and the burdens of snow in the branches of the trees grow and grow, until eventually these icy loads envelope their bearers.

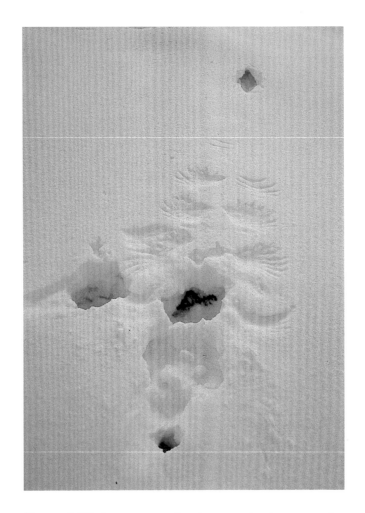

Signs of life in a snowy landscape, the burrow of a
black grouse and the tracks of a fox.

The snow in the branches is the inexorable force
that shapes the forests on the hilltops. Many of the
dead standing trunks and the flat-crowned or di-
vided trees are crushed beneath several tons of accu-
mulated snow.

It is in this environment, where the most tena-
cious of spruces and sturdiest of pines are brought
to the ground by their burdens of snow, that the
diminutive willow tit lives, a feathery bundle that
has to put up with night temperatures almost fifty
degrees below zero.

A silent, snowy forest, as if dead, can in fact be full of the most surprising living forms.

On the lengthening days following the solstice the tracks of hares seem to appear as if out of nowhere, for their makers prefer to move around under cover of dusk.

The lengthening day also tempts the squirrel to venture further afield.

And the increasing light sets the ravens off practicing their spring acrobatics in the air in spite of the biting cold.

By February, with the air still frosty, a miracle takes place. The glow of the sun releases the first branches of the trees from their burden of snow, although the water freezes again in a moment, and by evening at the latest, leaving crystal-clear icicles.

But the arc of the sun in the sky is lengthening from day to day, and the shadows forsake the valleys.

Still the clouds of snow billow over the hills and the dense storms ravage the forests, which otherwise have an air of the coming spring about them.

The light reflected from the cotton-wool of the snow arouses the Siberian tit, which has had a quiet time over the winter, and puts the Siberian jays in a playful mood.

An ancient eagle's nest buried beneath a thick bed of snow gains a new covering of twigs, offering prospects for the coming nesting season.

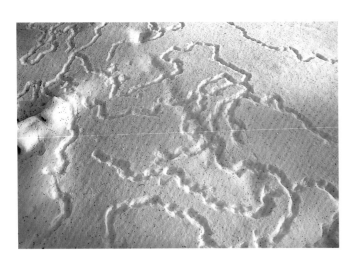

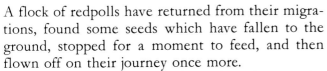

A flock of redpolls have returned from their migrations, found some seeds which have fallen to the ground, stopped for a moment to feed, and then flown off on their journey once more.

The willow grouse are able to hop about on the snow with quite different steps from those they had at the depths of the dark season, and the capercaillie's wings are brushing the snow as if in preparation for its spring jousting.

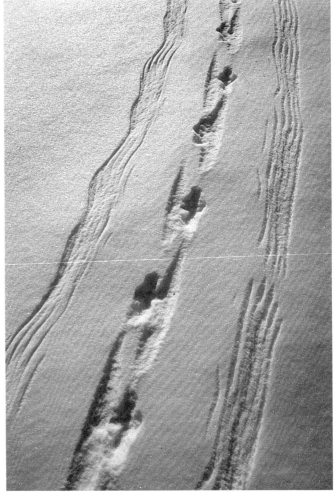

Night or day, the wolverine is always on the move.

A bear which has woken up early from its winter hibernation has come to the edge of a bog in search of its first meal. It finds the going easy as it pads across the crust of the snow.

A stream crossing a bog is already free of ice, but the wind is still blowing clouds of fine snow over the frozen lake.

A flock of returning snow buntings streaks across the clearings in the forest as if driven by the wind.

The hungry bear goes on with its search for food.

The winds are gradually bringing in the spring, although there are many snowstorms to come first.

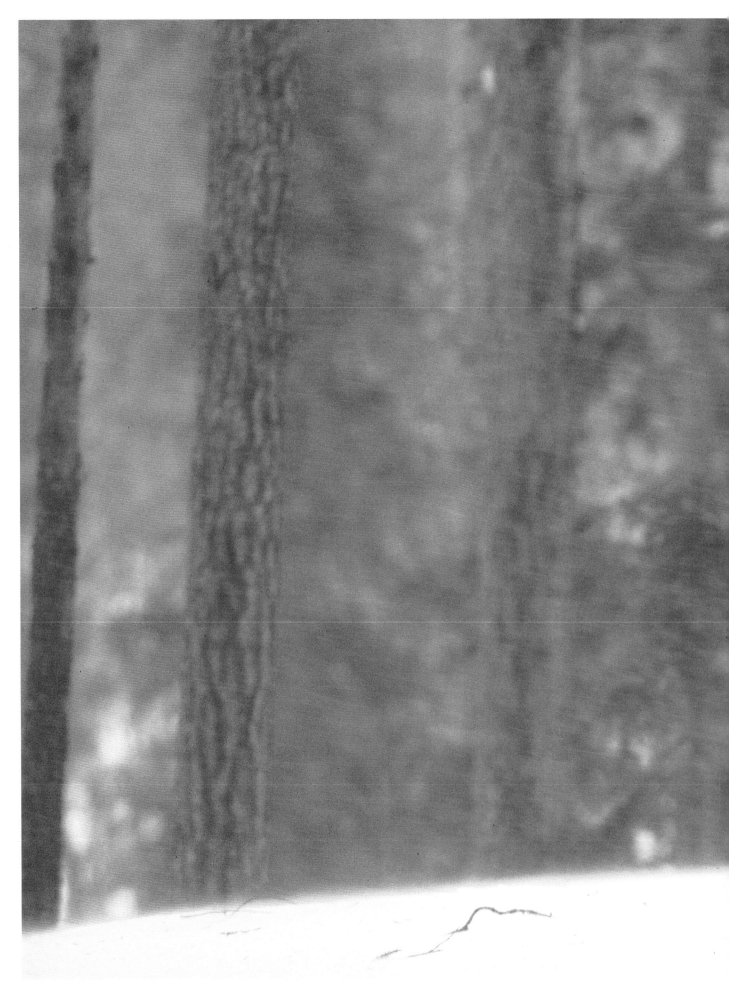

The bear's tribulations do not come to an end with the finding of a good carcass. Even if there are no other problems, there is at least a clever, although wary raven which will do everything it can to tease the huge visitor to its table.

It is over a carcass that the creatures of the taiga forest test their strength, authority and cunning against each other.

The eagle is the king of the winged predators, while a buzzard which has returned early from its migration has to fight for a place as an interloper at the ravens' dinner. The herring gull, veteran of the seas and rubbish tips, is a determined, fearless com-batant even for the experienced raven.

Meanwhile the great grey owl, which prefers voles to carrion, surveys the flat expanse of snow from its solitary vantage point on the edge of the forest.

The elk are on the move to their spring grazing grounds.

The male willow grouse keep up their noisy croaking on clear spring nights, marking out their territories, while the hens fly up onto the branches of the trees to feed greedily on the buds in preparation for the laying season.

The wolverine does well to follow the bear's movements. It usually leaves something behind for the smaller animals that come in its wake.

New falls of snow and spells of severe frost delay the coming of spring from time to time, but eventually the faster flowing streams and smaller lakes lose their cover of ice in places.

The goldeneye ducks that appear on the first patches of open water lay claim over their nesting territories as soon as they can. A couple of weeks later they are joined on the ponds in the forests by the smews, which make their nests in hollow trees.

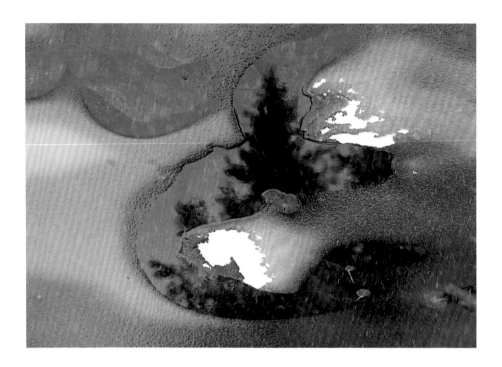

The young ravens have already hatched by the time the first wedge of cranes speeds across the sky towards the now rapidly thawing bogs.

The stretches of open water and flooded shores are suddenly alive with swans, geese, smaller ducks of all kinds, numerous waders and even gulls.

The huge crane, with its dignified presence and impressive movements stands out easily from the crowd of migratory brids, while the delicate, shy pintail duck catches the eye less often.

It takes a long time for the ice colonnades on the rock faces to melt. The flowing water gradually eats into the columns, but freezes at night to form new patterns.

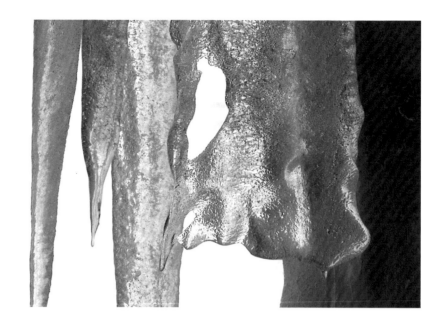

Finally the pillars dwindle away and are reduced to clinking slats of ice.

The forest prepares for its great purification, the spring floods.

The flood varies greatly with the vagaries of the spring weather, but sooner on later it will carry the last of the snow away.

The waters of the spring flood come to rest in the nearby lake, where thin, silvery fingers of ice are all that remain from the solid layer that covered it throughout the winter.

The last remnants of the ice break up, spin round, clink together and finally disappear in the heat of the sun.

Winter usually fights back a few times, in protest at the advancing spring, but the sight of a wagtail beside the new snow on an overhead wire is a further sign of the proximity of summer.

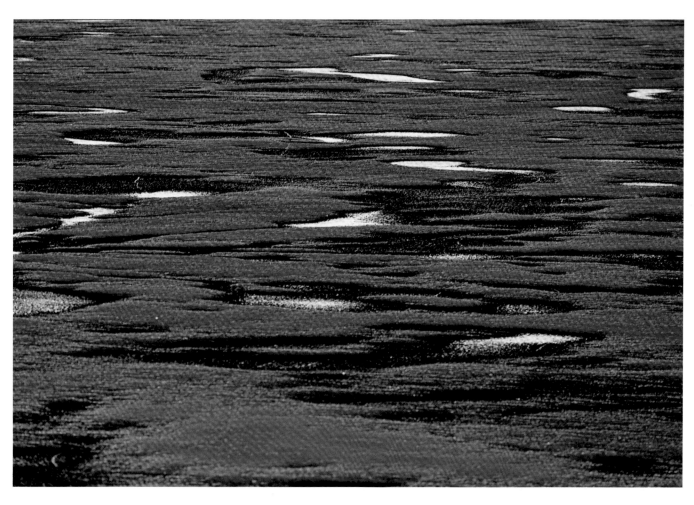

With the very last patches of snow lingering in the shade of the forests, the midges indulge in their first dance of the spring.

Winter in the taiga has given way to summer once more.